Babysitting Cal

A comedy

John H Newmeir

Samuel French—London
New York-Toronto-Hollywood

ISBN 978 0 573 12152 4

Please see page iv for further copyright information

BABYSITTING CALVIN

First performed by Adelphi Players at the Thurrock
Drama Festival on 11th June, 1997, with the following
cast:

Katie	Karin Ridgers
Calvin	Adam Popplewell
Donna	Angela Langford
Laura	Ann Newmeir
Bob	John H Newmeir

Directed by **John H Newmeir**

*Winner of the National Drama Festivals Association
(NDFA) George Taylor Memorial Award 1997/98*

CHARACTERS
(in order of appearance)

Katie, Calvin's mother, 20s
Calvin, 10-month-old baby (Laura's husband in his
   previous life—played by an adult)
Donna, Katie's friend, young
Laura, Calvin's former wife, 40s
Bob, Laura's "friend", 40s

The action of the play takes place in the living-room in
Katie's flat

Time: the present

SCENE 1: Early evening
SCENE 2: Two hours later

AUTHOR'S PRODUCTION NOTES

Understanding the limitations that some drama groups have to adhere to, I have tried to create simplicity and flexibility within the play.

Costumes, even Calvin's, should be simple to obtain and the setting is quite straightforward.

There is no hard and fast rule for you to copy my suggested furniture plot as the only items which are used are the cardboard box, telephone, sofa and play-pen. Feel free to establish your own influence, so long as you remain with the principle of a low budget apartment. However, be mindful to build the play-pen larger so as to accommodate an adult!

The characters themselves can be flexible. For instance—mothers come in all shapes, sizes and ages (with certain constraints). So it follows that Katie may be modified to suit the availability of your actresses. Likewise Laura etc. can be older or younger than as stated.

When ages are changed, careful consideration must be taken and other characters altered accordingly. For this purpose, the cast is divided into two categories: (a) Katie and Donna and (b) Laura, Bob and Calvin.

The essence of the play is fun for both cast and audience alike. As all good farces, and those comedies bordering on farce, are built on speed and energy, so it falls to Katie to initiate the pace from the outset. Behind schedule with a million and one things on her mind, the chasing around to catch up must appear frantic. Donna's appearance as the man-hungry companion is both pleasing to the eye and helps establish the sex-mad character of Bob. Laura's level-headedness is the only semblance of normality during the first scene and creates the "straight man" syndrome in the second. Calvin's character and general appearance are comical and care must be taken that he does not detract from other acting areas.

J. H. N.

BABYSITTING CALVIN

SCENE 1

Katie's living-room. Early evening

A large play-pen stands DL, *two thirds into the stage, with the remaining third off behind the curtain. Inside lie a nursery book, baby's rattle, small teddy bear and various coloured plastic bricks (of which two are red and two are yellow). Opposite, a telephone stands on a replica antique table with an address book close by. A sofa with cushions to match is* C, *while against the back wall a coat stand is positioned beside a large cardboard box housing some of Calvin's toys. Farther along, a standard lamp towers over a rocking chair, both of which are nestling neatly beside an inexpensive bookcase. Elsewhere other items of furniture complete the scene of a low budget but respectable flat*

The CURTAIN *rises on the living-room littered with baby toys, baby clothes and the strewn pages of a tabloid newspaper*

Katie, Calvin's young, pretty, single parent mum, enters UR. *She is wearing a full-length dressing gown, a pair of slippers and a towel wrapped around her hair. From her mannerisms it is obvious she is tense and somewhat behind schedule. She gathers the toys and throws them into the large box* UC. *Picking up the clothes, she ponders, then drops them in the box too*

Katie (*to herself*) I'll never be ready in time.

The phone rings and with great annoyance she lifts the receiver

(*Sharply*) Hallo. (*She moderates her voice*) Oh, hallo, Mother. ...
Was I? ... Well, I'm trying to get ready, the babysitter will be here
any moment. ... I told you last week that I was going out for a
drink with a friend. ... Yes, I did. ... Mother, I distinctly
remember telling you. ... No, a *girl*friend. (*She raises her
eyebrows and sighs*) What did you phone up for? (*Disinterestedly*)
Did he, how nice. ... I'm sure he did. ... I'm sure it was. ...
Mother, can we have this conversation some other time? ... Of
course I'm interested, it's just... Mother, I've got to go. ... No. ...
Yes. ... Yes. ... No. ... Of course not. ... Yes, I will. ... Goodbye
Mother. ... Goodbye. ... Mother, I'm going to put the phone
down. ... Goodbye. (*She replaces the receiver. To herself*) Ooh!
(*She reassembles the newspaper, unceremoniously dumps it on
the sofa and quickly picks up a few more toys, then suddenly
straightens up with horror*) The bathwater! Oh my God, I've left
it running!

Katie hurriedly exits UR

Pause

The phone rings again

(*Off*) Oh, bloody hell!

The phone continues to ring persistently

Eventually Katie rushes in from UR *with just a bath towel wrapped
around her in place of the dressing gown. She snatches up the
phone*

(*Abruptly*) What? ... No, Mother, we weren't cut off. ...
Everything's fine. ... I'm just trying very badly to get ready, in
fact I'm standing here with only a towel around me and I'm
getting as cold as the bathwater. ... Well, I'm sorry if I sound rude,
I don't mean to be. ... Of course I'm not mad at you. ... Honest
I'm not. ... Look, I'll phone you tomorrow. ... I promise I will.

... I know I don't always but I promise I will tomorrow. (*Frustrated*) Mother! ... Look I've got to go, I'll speak to you soon. ... No, I meant tomorrow. ... I did. ... It was a slip of the tongue. ... It *was*. ... All right, first thing in the morning. ... I will. ... Give my love to Dad. ... OK, bye. (*She replaces the receiver*) What was I doing? (*She looks down at herself*) Bathing. (*Towards the play-pen*) Be a good boy, Calvin. Mummy won't be long.

Katie exits UR

Calvin crawls on from DL *into the play-pen. He is in his late thirties to early forties and dressed as a baby, in an all-in-one romper suit topped by a motif of a teddy or panda. A dummy in his mouth is firmly attached to a ribbon around his neck and with concentration and determination he pulls himself up the frame of the play-pen, rests his arms on the edge, spits out his dummy and addresses the audience*

Calvin (*to the audience*) Phew. That's my mum. Lovely, isn't she? She's in a right old state though. Tonight's the first time she's been out on her own since I've been born. Haven't got a dad, he ran off and left her, so I'm the man of the house, or I will be when I grow up. And that won't be long 'cos I'm nearly ten months old already. Having a single parent, and being an only child, means I get spoilt something rotten. Only got to cry and I get whatever I want. Food, drink, toys, attention. Watch, I'll show you. (*Bending down he picks up his rattle, bangs it hard against his head and cries out loud*)

Katie rushes on from UR

Katie (*concerned*) What is it? What's wrong?

Calvin rubs his head and holds up the rattle

Oh, you silly boy, you've hurt yourself with that naughty rattle. (*She takes the rattle*) I'll smack it for you. (*She taps it lightly*)

There, there, Mummy's smacked that bad Mister Rattle. Now you stop crying and Mummy will make it all better. (*She bends down to rub his head and kisses the injured part*)

Calvin stops crying and winks at the audience

That's a good boy.

Katie crosses and exits UR, *still carrying the rattle*

Calvin (*to the audience*) Get the picture. 'Course, if I overdo it I finish up with a mouth full of gripe water, ugh! But I've got it off to a fine art now. Yes, life's a little bundle of joy, if you get my meaning. I'm Calvin by the way. (*He smiles angelically*) Named after some old French saint. It means "bald". (*He feels his hair*) Not that I'm either. Why couldn't she just call me Tommy? Like I was before. Oh yes, we babies can remember our previous life. Why do you think we look at you so knowingly and seem to understand every word? That's because we do. No, we don't forget until we're twelve months old, or start to speak, whichever comes first. That's why none of you can recall being pushed around in a pram. I had a lovely wife back then, Laura was her name. Always had to fight the men off ... especially Bob! He was my best friend. 'Course she always thought he was being nice, but I knew what he was after, and he wasn't going to get it while I was around. Unfortunately I died young. So you see, I want to remember everything as long as I can. I'm not saying anything until I have to. I'll just carry on with the baby gurgles and keep mum. (*He chuckles at his own joke*)

The doorbell rings. Calvin eases himself down and starts to play with some building blocks

Katie (*off*) Oh no! They're not here already. (*She shouts*) Just a minute.

Pause

Katie enters UR, *still wearing the towel covering her hair and a plain black dress unzipped at the back. She swiftly crosses and exits* UL

(*Off*) You're early. I'm not quite... Oh, it's you, Donna. Come in, I'm still finishing off.

The sound of the front door closing is heard off

Donna and Katie enter UL. *Donna is of similar age to her friend with very attractive features and an ample bosom. She is discreetly made-up and wearing a mini skirt, an expensive-looking see-through blouse and black tights. All in all, she is dressed to kill*

Donna Who else are you expecting?
Katie The babysitter.
Donna (*twirling*) Like the blouse? Reduced from forty-five to thirty pounds up in town.
Katie I wish I could afford thirty pounds. Where's your coat?
Donna In the car. I don't think I'll need it tonight, do you?
Katie (*slightly depressed*) Could you zip me up, please. (*She turns round*)

Donna fastens Katie's dress

(*Turning back*) Do I look all right?
Donna (*somewhat unconvincing*) Smashing.
Katie I feel so plain.
Donna Don't talk daft. (*She moves forward to a mirror situated on the "fourth wall" and adjusts her make-up and hair while at the same time admiring herself*) Anyway, it's no good using the same bait as me. You wouldn't want the kind of fish I'm after.
Katie I wouldn't mind any kind of fish.
Donna You need to attract the homely guy. The one that won't flinch or run away when you tell them you've got a kid. Whereas I need to attract a completely——

Katie Yes, I think I get the picture. I've just got to finish my hair, I'll only be two ticks. Will you be all right?

Donna You carry on. I'll go and give a big hug and kiss to my favourite godson.

Katie begins to move above the sofa as Calvin looks towards the audience with a big smile of anticipation on his face

How is he?

Katie Fine. He's playing quietly at the moment. Let's hope he behaves for the sitter.

Donna Of course he will. He's a little angel.

Katie He's not so little any more. He's grown quite a bit since you last saw him.

Donna moves towards the play-pen

Don't pick him up, will you. I want him settled before I go out.

Katie exits UR

Donna leans over and pulls Calvin's head into her bosom, kissing his head

Calvin (*to the audience in total bliss*) I don't ever want to grow up.

Donna I'll tell you what. You weren't kidding when you said he'd grown.

Katie (*off*) Told you.

Donna What are you putting in his bottle—Guinness? (*She addresses Calvin with baby talk*) Hallo den. And how's my Calvy walvy?

He looks up at her, smiles and gurgles a reply

Are you trying to talk to your favourite Auntie Donna? (*To Katie*) I think he's trying to talk.

Katie (*off*) He does, but nothing comes out.

Donna Say Mum. Mum… Mum… Mum.

He stops smiling and stares at her

Mum… Mum… Mum. Calvy say it. Mmmum.
Calvin (*to the audience*) Not a chance.
Donna Dadda. Calvin say Dadda. Oh no, you haven't got one, have you? Forget I said that.

He holds up a red brick

A red brick, there's a clever boy. Say red. R-r-r-ed.

He holds up a yellow brick with his other hand

That's a yellow one. 'Lellow. L-e-l-l-o-w.

He bangs them together

(*To Katie*) He's definitely trying to talk to me.

Katie enters UR, *brushing her hair*

Katie He does that a lot. It's his way of communicating. He's just lazy when it comes to using words. Almost there, only got to find my shoes and I'll be with you.

Katie exits UR

Donna gently takes the bricks away from Calvin

Donna And that's a noise, we mustn't do that. You have to play with them nicely. Look, build them up one on top of the other. Calvin do it.

Calvin watches intently at first and then knocks them down. He then picks two up and starts to bang them together again, this time with greater energy

No. What did Auntie Donna just say … that's a noise. (*She reaches out to take the bricks away*)

He slams her finger in between the bricks and laughs aloud

Now that wasn't very nice, was it? You hurt your Auntie Donna. Auntie Donna's going to cry.

Katie (*off*) What's he doing?

Donna Banging his bricks together.

Katie (*off*) He does that when he's happy.

Donna He must have a mean streak in him then.

The doorbell rings

Katie (*off*) That'll be the babysitter.

Donna I'll answer it, you finish getting ready.

Katie (*off*) Thanks. I'm nearly done.

Donna crosses and exits UL *as Calvin slowly hauls himself up the frame*

Calvin (*to the audience*) Here's my date for the evening. Hope she's like Auntie Donna. I'll be so well-behaved that I'll make her bounce me on her knee and snuggle me up all night long. Auntie Donna's lovely. My Mum's lovely too, but not like Auntie Donna. Why do we have to keep calling everybody Auntie or Uncle? It gets so confusing. And all that silly talk! "Calvy Walvy" and "lellow" for yellow. And if you think that's bad, you should hear my Mum's favourite… "Binkil Bumps". I ask you. I hate it when she calls me that. No wonder us babies take a year or more to talk. (*With a cheeky giggle*) Well, most of us, anyway.

Donna (*off*) Hallo, come in.

Slight pause

Go through.

Calvin (*to the audience*) Better get down now. I'll ignore them and play quietly, and be so cute when she comes over that she won't want to put me to bed early. That way I can stay up with her. Just me and the sitter—alone. (*He climbs down and becomes absorbed in his bricks*)

The sound of the front door shutting is heard off

Laura and Bob enter UL, *followed by Donna. Laura is in her early to mid forties with long blonde hair, slimmish and pleasing to the eye. Bob is a little older, possibly late forties, wearing a smart, expensive suit and shirt with co-ordinated tie. He holds a carrier bag containing four cans of lager and a bottle of wine which protrudes significantly from the bag. From the outset he finds it extremely difficult to avert his eyes from Donna*

Donna Katie will be here in a minute, she's just doing her hair. I'm Donna.
Bob (*eagerly*) I'm Bob.
Laura (*quietly in his ear*) Down boy.

Katie enters UR, *carrying her shoes*

Katie Sorry about that. Hallo, Laura, how are you?
Laura Fine, thanks. This is Bob, I hope you don't mind. He's offered to keep me company tonight.
Katie Of course I don't. (*She shakes his hand*) Pleased to meet you, Bob. This is Donna, who's hoping to lead me astray this evening.

They acknowledge each other

Take your coats off and make yourselves at home. Would you like a coffee?

Bob is transfixed by Donna

Bob No thanks, not for me. It's not my cup of tea.

Katie gives Laura a strange look

Laura Take no notice of him, he doesn't know what he's saying half the time. (*To Bob*) Katie asked if you'd like a coffee.

Bob Not for me. (*He shows the carrier bag*) I'm a lager man.

Laura (*removing her coat*) I had one before I came out, thanks all the same.

Donna Can I use your loo before we go?

Katie Of course you can. You know where it is, don't you?

Donna I'll find it. Shall I take the coats?

Katie Would you—thanks.

Donna takes Laura's coat, moving upstage deliberately and seductively and hangs it on the coat stand. She then gracefully crosses and exits UR, *fully aware that Bob is watching her every move, who in turn is unaware that Laura is watching him*

Bob Seems a nice girl.

Laura I think you mean big.

Bob I never said that.

Laura You didn't have to, your eyes told me. You can put them back now. (*To Katie*) So, where's the baby then?

Katie crosses to the sofa to put her shoes on. Bob moves above the sofa, peering off lecherously after Donna. During the following, he drifts aimlessly along the back of the sofa, finishing in front where he notices the newspaper. Placing his bag DL, *he sits and begins reading—page three first and then the sports pages*

Katie Over there in his play-pen.

Laura (*turning towards him*) Oh, he's gorgeous! Sorry, what did you say his name was?

Katie Calvin.

Laura (*towards Calvin*) That's a nice name ... friendly. (*Slightly taken aback*) How old did you say he was?

Katie Ten months.

Laura He's a big baby! What did he weigh at birth?

Katie (*rising*) Nearly twelve pounds.

Laura Wow! It's enough to put you off for life.

Katie (*crossing*) I don't need anything to put me off. Trust me, there's not going to be any more. Besides, he's all I want.

Laura He's lovely though. (*To Calvin*) Hallo, Calvin. Are you going to be good for me tonight?

Bob (*aside*) And go to bed early.

Calvin stops playing and looks towards the audience

Calvin (*to the audience*) I know that voice. It can't be! (*He looks at Laura*) It is! (*To the audience*) It's Laura … my wife! (*With tremendous enthusiasm and a beaming smile he stretches out both arms to be picked up*)

Katie Oh, look, Laura, he's pleased to see you. I think you've made a hit there.

Laura Does he talk?

Katie Not a word. Although he's got nearly all his teeth.

Laura Can I hold him?

Katie It's up to you, but I warn you. Once he gets picked up, it's the Devil's own job to get him to sleep.

Calvin bangs his bricks together and then stands up against the side of the pen, shaking it vigorously

Bob (*with ulterior motive*) And we don't want that, do we?

Laura Maybe later then. (*To Bob*) Come and look at the baby, Bob.

Calvin (*to the audience, expressionless*) Bob!

Laura He's all excited. He likes me.

Calvin (*horrified*) Did she say *Bob*!?

Bob strolls over with great apathy, watched by the other two

Laura (*to Katie*) He's not a baby person.

Katie Most men aren't.

Bob (*unconvincing*) Very nice.

Laura Is that all you can say?

Bob What do you want me say?

Katie (*pacifying*) It's all right, Laura.

The three adults strike up a low mumbled conversation between themselves as Calvin stops shaking the play-pen and turns with horror upon his face

Calvin (*to the audience*) Bob! I might've known. As soon as my back is turned. What's she doing with him? Can't she see what he's like? He's never been any different. And what's worse is I'll have to call him Uncle. Well, I'm not having that. (*He turns to Bob and begins to cry heartily*)
Laura Now see what you've done. You've scared him. (*To Calvin*) There … there. Don't cry. (*She waves Bob away*) Nasty man's gone away.
Calvin (*to the audience*) I wished. (*He turns back and continues to cry*)
Laura (*placing the teddy in his arms*) Here. Hold teddy.
Katie He loves that bear.

Calvin throws the teddy violently across the stage in temper. All eyes follow the flight of the bear, but as Bob looks back he discovers the women's glare is focused firmly upon him

Bob What? What did I do?
Katie (*reassuringly*) Nothing, Bob. He's not used to men, that's all.
Laura Well, he doesn't like *you*. (*To Calvin*) Don't you like your Uncle Bobby then?

Calvin's crying intensifies

Bob (*pleading*) I didn't do anything.
Laura You didn't have to. Babies know who they like and who doesn't like them. It's a sixth sense they've got.

Katie starts towards the kitchen off R

Katie I'll get him some gripe water. That usually does the trick.

Terrified at the thought, Calvin reacts to this suggestion and

immediately ceases crying, sits down and begins playing with his
bricks. Katie stops and turns around slowly

Calvin (*to the audience, contemptuously*) He's not worth it.
Katie Told you. Not his favourite tipple.
Laura (*astonished*) It's almost as if he knew.

Calvin looks towards the audience and raises his eyebrows

Katie (*crossing* R) You'd better come through to the kitchen and I'll
show you where everything is. Baby's feed, nappies, etc.
Laura (*following her*) Does he still have a bottle?
Katie Yes. I've already made it up. All you've got to do is warm
it through when he's ready.

Laura and Katie exit DR *as Donna reappears* UR

Calvin begins to stare at Bob

Donna Where have they gone?
Bob (*crossing to the sofa*) Kitchen. Baby talk I believe. All the do's
and don'ts.
Donna What was Calvin crying for?
Bob (*sitting*) Apparently I upset him, but I didn't do anything. He
doesn't like me.
Donna You're imagining it.
Bob Am I? Look at him. He's just staring at me.
Donna (*sitting beside him*) He's fascinated by you—and I can't say
I blame him.
Bob (*preening himself*) Really.
Donna (*rubbing against him*) It's a shame you're Laura's boyfriend.
All the best are taken.
Bob (*responding*) I wouldn't strictly call myself her boyfriend.
Donna (*interested*) You wouldn't?
Bob No. We go back a long way, that's all. As she keeps reminding
me ... we're just friends.
Donna (*moving closer and placing a hand on his knee*) How good
a friend?

Bob begins getting hot under the collar

Bob The odd meal here and there, perhaps the occasional barbeque. Nothing out of the ordinary. In fact, tonight's the first time we've ever been alone together.

Donna (*slowly moving her hand up his leg*) I see.

Bob You do? I mean, do you?

Donna (*seductively*) Well, if the babysitting gets too boring... I could do with a "friend".

Bob You could? I mean, could you?

Donna (*running her fingers through his hair*) She's a lucky girl. All I can offer is soft lights, slow music and a hot, *hot* body.

Bob (*gulping*) I hate babies, all they're good for is crying, winding and you know what. It goes in one end and comes out the other. What's the point of them, they can't do anything. Mind you, babies don't like me much.

Donna And Laura?

Bob Who?

Her hand travels around his neck playing with his ear

Donna You're good, I'll give you that. The babysitter—your "friend".

Bob More boring than the baby. (*He looks nervously towards the kitchen*) Definitely more boring. Come to think of it, she's not really been interested in me since her husband died.

Donna And before he died?

Calvin leans forward, straining to hear his reply

Bob Oh no, nothing like that.

Donna (*taking her hands away*) You've disappointed me. I had you down for a man of action.

Bob (*quickly recovering*) Although I must admit, I did try it on once or twice.

Calvin's face becomes severe

Donna I knew my instincts were right about you. I'm not usually wrong.

Bob (*placing his arm around her*) And what are they telling you now?

Donna Don't you know?

Bob I've a shrewd idea.

Donna So what happened when you tried it on with her?

Bob Married! The faithful type—very dull woman really. Then she was too upset when he— (*he looks skyward*) you know.

Donna She can't be that dull, otherwise you wouldn't be with her tonight.

Bob (*cockily*) I thought I'd give her one more chance.

Donna In that case you'd better be careful she doesn't come in and catch you ... your "friend" that is.

Bob (*without conviction*) I'm not her property. (*He takes his arm away*) But I suppose she doesn't know that, and we don't want to ruin Katie's night, do we?

Donna What about her husband?

Bob Tommy? He never knew how devoted she was to him—the little weasel.

Calvin starts shaking the play-pen vehemently

(*Alarmed*) Now what's the matter with him?

Donna Probably ravenous like me. (*She rises*) I'll go and see if his feed's due.

Bob Er ... what about ... you know.

Donna (*teasing*) As I said, if it all gets too much—you know where you can find me ... don't you? (*She crosses enticingly towards the kitchen*)

Bob leaps to his feet

Bob (*desperate*) I don't.

Donna (*turning with an alluring smile*) Then you'd better try Macey's nightclub ... hadn't you?

Donna winks at him and exits into the kitchen

Bob (*excitedly to himself*) Yes. (*Calling after her*) Where's the toilet?

Donna (*off*) Down the hall, second on the left.

> *Bob crosses excitedly with a spring in his step and exits down the hallway*

> *Calvin stops shaking the play-pen*

Calvin (*to the audience*) He's sex mad! First Auntie Laura and now Auntie Donna. What am I saying? This Auntie business has definitely gotta stop, it's driving me crackers. That's my wife he's talking about. And I never knew he'd tried it on. (*With venom*) He'd better not tonight. Two-timing rat! I told you what he was like, didn't I? Why can't he just leave her be. Auntie Donna's more his style. Wait a minute, that gives me an idea. If I go to bed like a good boy and sleep through and Auntie Laura remains faithful like he said she has, then things around here will become boring. And if that's the case, Uncle Bobby will go and find Auntie Donna. Which will leave me all alone with Auntie Laura. Good old Auntie Donna. They say God works in mysterious ways. Well, she is my godmother, after all.

> *Bob enters UR carrying a rattle, which he tosses on to the sofa as he passes. He takes a few tentative steps forward, looks towards the kitchen and moves over to the play-pen*

Bob (*to Calvin*) Hallo then, old mate. Now, you've got to be a good boy for me tonight.

> *Calvin smiles and gurgles with delight*

I want you to go to sleep and not make a sound—all night.

> *Again Calvin gurgles and waves his arms with joy*

Because your Auntie Laura and me want to be alone. Grown-ups need their privacy sometimes to do things that little babies shouldn't see.

Calvin stops waving his arms

Your Auntie has been by herself for a long time now and she needs my company. It's like this, when Aunties have been— unaccompanied—shall we say for any length of time, they develop needs. And in the right place at the right time, bad Uncles help them with those needs. Tonight is one of those times— (*aside*) I hope. And as I'm so good at being bad, my aim is to please. So, as I said, you be a good little boy, because your bad Uncle Bobby Wobby has a little surprise for your nice Auntie Laura. (*He produces a packet of contraceptives from his jacket pocket, dangling them in front of Calvin*) Now, not a word. (*He pops the dummy into Calvin's mouth*) Put your dummy in, behave yourself and don't play me up.

Calvin looks directly at the audience in astonishment at first and then his face turns to devilment as Bob replaces the package in his jacket pocket and wanders up to the sofa, singing "Tell Laura I love her"

Black-out

SCENE 2

Two hours later

Some of baby toys from the large box have found their way back on to the floor, including some of the bricks from the play-pen. R *of the sofa is a wine glass beside the now empty bottle of wine, and two empty lager cans are* L

Calvin is positioned behind the sofa, hidden from view

As the Lights come up, Bob removes his suit jacket and lays it neatly

over the side of the play-pen. During the following action, his
movement is brisk and excitable with constant anxious glances
towards the hall. Loosening his tie, he half rolls his shirt sleeves,
unfastens three buttons and crosses to the mirror where he combs
his hair and admires himself vainly

Bob (*to himself*) Maybe another button. (*He unfastens another*
button, widens the shirt, revealing his chest, and stands posing,
examining the effect)

Pause

Perfect. (*Satisfied with his appearance, he crosses* R *of the sofa*
and steps out of his shoes, then moves towards the hall and dims
the lights. Turning to the play-pen, he extracts a small portable
cassette player from the inside pocket of his jacket and switches
it on) Some romantic music accompanied with soft lights to set
the mood.

Quiet romantic music, almost inaudible with a tinny effect, is heard.
Hooking the player to the same pocket, he then removes a small roll-
on deodorant from one of the side pockets, which he applies under
both arms. He replaces the deodorant and takes out a bottle of
aftershave, splashing it over his chest liberally and dabbing behind
each ear. From the other pocket he produces a breath freshener
spray, giving three short puffs into his mouth

Smell nice, taste nice, and be nice. Mix it with atmosphere and a
bottle of wine, which she's already drunk, and the night's mine.
(*He turns his attention to the top pocket*) And the final *pièce de*
résistance. (*He brandishes a packet of contraceptives*) *Voilà!*
The vital ingredient for the ultimate protection. Be prepared,
that's what I say. Leave nothing to chance. I enjoyed those boy
scout days, they taught me such a lot. (*He moves up to the sofa*)
Now, which cushion? Centre, I think. (*He places the packet under*
the centre cushion and straightens up the others to remove any
suspicion)

Laura enters from the hallway

Laura He's fast asleep, bless him. Why have you turned the lights down?

Bob (*sitting on the sofa*) Because if he wakes up and sees the light on full, he'll want to come out, and I've also put some soothing background music on for him.

Laura That's very sweet of you, Bob. You can be so thoughtful at times.

Bob (*patting the cushion*) I try to think of everything.

Laura sits on Bob's right

Laura (*sniffing*) Have you put aftershave on?

Bob commences his seduction technique on Laura, believing it to be impressive but in truth creating little or no effect on her

Bob Not recently. A small droplet before I left home, just to close the pores, you understand. Why?

Laura (*casually*) Only wondered.

Bob (*moving close*) Irresistible, isn't it?

Laura It's very strong.

Bob That's the heat. Confined spaces and (*he moves even closer*) close contact cause the aromatic fragrance to become intoxicating.

Laura (*edging slightly away*) Certainly overpowering.

Bob Then you like it?

Laura Not particularly. What is it?

Bob "Courageous", fifty pounds for just a tiny bottle, (*he moves closer*) very hard to come by, you know, you can't just get it in any old shop.

Laura I believe you. (*She tries to move away again, but is trapped at the end of the sofa*)

Bob It can only be truly appreciated by those who find familiarity an enjoyable amusement. In a little while you'll feel completely different about it.

Laura I doubt it, not if you put it on at home. That was almost three
hours ago. It's had all the time it needs to settle down.
Bob Ah, but you're forgetting it's been re-stimulated by the heat.
Laura What heat? It's not that warm in here.
Bob I'm talking of body heat, Laura. (*He places his arm around
her*) *Your* body heat to be precise.
Laura Mine? But I feel cold.
Bob (*placing his other hand on her knee*) That's nerves.
Laura (*slapping his hand*) What have I got to be nervous about?
And what have you been eating? Garlic?
Bob (*slightly offended*) No, I haven't!
Laura (*pushing him away*) Your breath's all spicy.
Bob You're doing this on purpose, aren't you?
Laura Doing what?
Bob Pretending I smell.
Laura But you do!
Bob Charming! Thanks a lot.
Laura Not bodily.
Bob It happens to be a freshen-up mouth spray.
Laura Well, I never knew, did I? (*She holds his hand*) Sorry, Bob.
I didn't mean it to come out as it sounded—still friends?
Bob Laura, can't we be more than friends?
Laura (*taking her hand away*) Now don't start that again, Bob.
We've been through all this. You know my feelings.
Bob That was before.
Laura Nothing's changed.

Slight pause

Bob changes tactics and attacks where she is most vulnerable

Bob Tommy wouldn't want you to remain all by yourself. He'd
want you to enjoy yourself, live life to the full—find someone
else.
Laura How do you know?
Bob Because he told me.
Laura When?

Bob We often used to talk about such things. Many a time he'd say to me "Bob, if anything ever happens to me, I wouldn't want my Laura to face life by herself".

Laura And he nominated you, I suppose?

Bob As a matter of fact he did. "Look after her, Bob" he said. "You're the only one I know she'd be happy with".

Laura (*uncertain*) Honestly? Did he really say that?

Bob His very words. That's why I've always been there for you.

Laura I can't argue with that.

Bob For Tommy. I did it for Tommy, because that's how he wanted it. I know he'd be very happy if we got together.

Laura We are together.

Bob You know what I mean. What do you say, eh? For Tommy's sake.

Laura I'd have to think about it.

Bob What is there to think about? Aren't I kind?

Laura Yes.

Bob (*placing his arm around her*) Thoughtful?

Laura Yes.

Bob (*sliding his other arm around her waist*) Considerate?

Laura Yes.

Bob (*leaning over her*) Generous?

Laura Yes.

Bob Well, then. (*He pushes her down on the sofa*) Oh Laura. (*He clambers all over her in a frenzied and excited state*)

Laura, in contrast, is completely uninterested in his advances and struggles hard to control his ardour—but to little avail. Bob's hands seem to be everywhere and she has great difficulty keeping him at bay

Laura Ouch!

Bob (*without relenting*) What is it?

Laura There's something digging in my back. You'll have to get up.

Bob It's only the cushion. Don't worry about it.

Laura It's not the cushion.

Bob Then it's a spring. Come on, don't stop, you'll lose the
moment.
Laura I haven't had the moment, and I don't want it anyway. (*She
removes a baby's rattle from behind her*) It's a rattle. No wonder
it hurt.

Bob slowly runs his free hand up her leg

Bob Oh Laura... I love you.
Laura (*hitting his hand with the rattle*) Don't be so ridiculous, Bob.
Bob I do. I do.
Laura Can you get off me? This has gone far enough.
Bob No it hasn't, we've still a way to go.
Laura Bob, can you get off please, you're hurting. Bob! *Bob!* (*She
shouts*) BOB!

The sound of a baby crying is heard from off L

Bob Now you've woken the baby.
Laura He's probably hungry. I told you not to put him down until
after he was fed.
Bob Don't move. He might go back off.

*They both lie perfectly motionless for a few seconds, but the crying
persists*

Laura It's no good, he's not going to stop. I'll have to go in to him.
Bob (*sitting back*) Just give him his bottle then. You won't need to
stay in there. He's quite capable of holding it himself.
Laura (*rising*) I'll go and see. He might just want his dummy.
Bob (*aside*) I should be so lucky.

Laura crosses L

Laura And turn that awful noise off.

Switching the lights on to full, Laura exits down the hallway

Bob (*to himself*) That's the trouble with babysitting—the bloody babies. If it wasn't for them it'd be great. (*He rises and crosses to his jacket*) I wouldn't mind, but she was just getting in the mood. (*Removing the cassette player, he switches off the music, moves back to the sofa and extracts the packet from behind the cushion*) Nearly. Don't worry, your time will come. I'll have her begging me by the end of the evening.

Laura enters from the hall, carrying "Calvin" in her arms, represented by a large baby doll wrapped in a blanket and hidden from audience view

Bob quickly thrusts the packet back under the cushion

(*Surprised*) What have you brought him out here for?
Laura Because he needs changing, he's hungry and he's wide awake. That's why.
Bob You're not gonna change him in front of me, are you? I don't like that sort of thing.
Laura It's a baby, Bob.
Bob I don't care. It all smells the same.
Laura I feel like that about certain aftershaves.
Bob (*ignoring her remark*) Can't you do it outside?
Laura Bob, you can't change a baby outside!
Bob It's not very nice doing it in here in front of me, is it?
Laura Well, fetch me a clean nappy and I'll do it behind the sofa while you go and get him some food. It's on the side in the kitchen on a plastic dish. It may have cooled off by now. If so, put it on a plate and warm it through in the microwave.

Bob reluctantly crosses DR

Warm, I said, not boiling ... and don't forget his spoon.

Bob exits into the kitchen

(*To "Calvin"*) Isn't he a silly billy? What do you think of him?

"Calvin" blows a loud raspberry

I'm not so sure which end that came from, but I agree with you all the same.

Bob returns with a basket of nappy change items including a, as yet, hidden bottle of gripe water and immediately returns to the kitchen

Laura bends down behind the sofa with "Calvin", disappearing from view. Slight pause

There's a messy nappy.
Bob (*off*) I can smell it.

Longer pause

Laura Lay still, there's a good boy. Auntie Laura's not done this for a long time. ... No, leave the talcum powder alone. ... Calvin. ... Play with the clean one, not the dirty nappy. ... Now you've put your hand in it... Give me your little handy and I'll make it clean again. I wish you could talk. Wouldn't it be nice if you said your first word for when Mummy got back.

Slight pause

All done. I'll just get rid of this nasty nappy wappy before grumpy old Uncle Bobby comes back.

Laura rises and exits UR

Calvin pops his head out from behind the sofa

Calvin (*to the audience*) Change of plan. (*He crawls* DC) He's not finding this boring at all. He's enjoying himself. Well, not with my wife he's not. I heard Auntie Laura scream out, because I wasn't really asleep, I was just pretending. And I've got a good idea why she did. (*Slight pause*) Took a lot to mess my nappy, shame he didn't see my efforts. I'll just have to make him play with me, or go find Auntie Donna in that nightclub. (*Angelically*) Aren't I nice?

Bob enters DR *with a plastic dish of baby food and a spoon*

Bob This looks disgusting. (*He looks around*) Where's she gone?

Calvin sits back and waves his outstretched arms in anticipation

Hungry, are you? (*He looks around again*) I suppose the sooner you're fed the quicker you'll get to bed. Come on, over here. (*He sits on the sofa*)

Calvin crawls beside him. Bob starts to feed him and at first all is well

Come on, eat faster.

Suddenly Calvin grabs the spoon

No. That's naughty.

Looking first at the food, then at Bob, Calvin throws it into Bob's face, then grabs two bricks and bangs them together with joy

Placing the food and spoon on the floor, Bob jumps up, mumbling some unpleasantries, takes a handkerchief from his pocket and exits into the kitchen DR, *wiping his face*

Calvin (*to the audience*) This is just the beginning. (*He crawls towards the play-pen, pushing the dish and spoon along*)

Laura enters UR *as Bob enters* DR

*During the next interchange of dialogue, Calvin, unnoticed, starts
spreading his food with the spoon all down Bob's jacket*

Bob Look what he's done.
Laura What?
Bob Thrown his dinner in my face, that's what.
Laura He didn't mean it. He's only a baby, you have to expect this
sort of thing.
Bob (*sarcastically*) It was an accident, was it? He was aiming for
the wall, I suppose.
Laura You shouldn't let him play with his food.
Bob I didn't. He just grabbed it.
Laura Because you weren't paying attention. You can't afford to
take your eyes away for one second.
Bob You feed him then, if you're so clever. You're the babysitter.
Laura Where's his dish?

*They both look across and are mortified to discover the atrocity
Calvin has created, decorating the jacket with his food*

Bob (*horrified*) My jacket! (*He races across and snatches the
jacket away*)
Laura (*frightened*) Bob, be careful! You'll frighten him.
Bob (*holding up the jacket*) Look at it. It's ruined.
Laura It's not ruined. (*She picks up the food and spoon*) Give it to
me and I'll sponge it down. (*She exchanges the dish and spoon for
the coat and crosses* R) You finish feeding him.

Laura exits DR

Bob (*quietly*) I'll finish him all right. (*He sits back on the sofa*)
Come here you little sod. Din dins.

Calvin remains motionless

Don't play me about, I'm not in the mood.

Calvin continues to stare at him ominously

Suit yourself. You'll be hungry, not me.

Pause

(*Feeling uncomfortable*) Will you stop staring at me like that?
Laura (*off*) How's it going?
Bob What do you think?
Laura (*off*) Soon as you've finished we can put him down again.

Misunderstanding her meaning, Bob quickly picks up the spoon and dish

Bob (*to himself*) That sounds promising. (*To Calvin*) Get over here
and eat this, do you hear me? (*Through his teeth*) Or one of us will
have a sore arse.

Calvin is unmoved by this threat. Bob decides to change tactics and pretends to eat the food

Mmm ... lovely.

Calvin still refuses to budge

You really are the most irritating...
Laura (*off*) Is he eating it?
Bob He will. (*To himself*) If Mohammed won't go to the mountain...
(*He kneels down beside Calvin, offering the spoon*)

Calvin repeatedly turns his head away in absolute defiance. Exasperated, Bob decides to show what he's missing and offers the spoon to his own lips, whereupon Calvin leans forward and pushes it in

Ugh! (*He spits it on to the carpet*) It's worse than it looks.

*While he's doubled over, Calvin grabs a large clump of hair with
both hands and tugs up and down and side to side as Bob screams
in pain*

Laura! *Laura!* LAURA!

Laura rushes in from DR

Laura What's going on?
Bob Get him off! He's got my bloody hair.

Moving across L, *she releases Calvin's hand and he sits back,
gurgling happily*

Laura He's only playing. See, he's laughing.
Bob (*rubbing his head*) Let him play with your hair then.
Laura I don't know who the bigger baby is. You or him.
Bob (*rising*) Why don't you put him to bed? He's obviously not
    hungry.
Laura He's wide awake. If I lay him in his cot, he won't go off, and
    then I'll be traipsing in and out all evening. Why don't you play
    with him for a while, try and tire him out.
Bob (*flabbergasted*) Play with him? (*Sarcastically*) Let's see,
    we've already played throw the food, ruin the jacket and pull the
    hair. Oh dear, I seem to have exhausted my full range of baby
    party games. Any suggestions?
Laura There's plenty to choose from in his toy box. Or what about
    his bricks? Build him something and see if he can copy it.
Bob That's hardly going to tire him out.
Laura How about his teddy? Apparently he loves that.
Bob (*appalled*) I'm not playing with no teddy.
Laura Put him on your back then, and play horses. That's bound
    to exhaust him.
Bob Are you mad! He'll break every bone in my spine. He weighs
    a ton.

*Calvin bobs up and down with excitement, banging two bricks
together in approval*

Laura Too late.
Bob What do you mean "too late"?
Laura He's heard us.
Bob He doesn't know what we're saying. He's only ten months old, for Christsake!

As they both look across at Calvin, he puts the bricks down and begins miming horse riding and making an incomprehensible sound very similar to "gee gee"

Laura You were saying?
Bob That's incredible! There's something weird about this kid.
Laura Because he wants a ride on your back? Don't be daft.
Bob How many ten-month-old kids can do what he just did?
Laura Katie probably does it with him all the time. He obviously understands the odd word like "back" or "horses".

Responding on cue, Calvin repeats his mime act

See, what did I say?
Bob There's something very peculiar about that kid. I can't place it but I can feel it.
Laura It's called intelligence. Maybe that's why you can't place it.
Bob Very funny. No, it's something else. I can't quite put my finger on it.
Laura *(flippantly)* Let me know when you figure it out. It sounds intriguing. Meanwhile, I'll be getting his bottle ready.

Laura exits DR, leaving Bob studying Calvin as he crawls to him and pulls at his trouser leg

Bob *(calling after her)* And put half a dozen sleeping pills in. *(To Calvin)* I suppose you do want to play this silly game?

Calvin claps his hands together

I thought you might. Well, if it'll get you to bed early. *(He grudgingly goes down on to his hands and knees)*

*Calvin happily crawls over and strives to climb on Bob's back.
Unable to do so after several attempts, he begins crying
uncontrollably*

Laura enters DR *with a baby's bottle in her hand*

Laura (*worried*) What have you done?
Bob (*dismayed*) I haven't done anything. He just started crying.
Laura (*bending down to cuddle Calvin*) What were you doing
    before?
Bob Nothing.
Laura It must have been something. Babies don't just cry for
    nothing.
Bob He does. (*He demonstrates the action*) Look, all I did was to
    go down on my hands and knees to give him a ride like you said,
    and the next thing I knew he was howling in my ear.
Laura (*realizing*) No wonder he's crying, he couldn't get on. Look
    at the size of you to him. You have to lie flat first and come up
    gradually. Haven't you got any sense?
Bob (*aside*) If I did I wouldn't be doing this.
Laura Go on then, lie down.
Bob (*irritably*) All right, all right. No need to rush.
Laura (*to Calvin*) There you are, you can get on now.

*Bob lies prostrate on the floor, as Laura "helps" Calvin climb on
to his back. Bob feels the weight*

Bob Ooh! ...Fat lump. (*He struggles to rise on to his knees, feeling
    the strain, and with extreme effort and difficulty slowly begins
    walking around*)

*Laura watches closely. After a few seconds she moves up and sits on
the edge of the sofa. Calvin starts to bounce up and down, causing
Bob great distress and Laura becomes concerned for the baby's
safety*

Laura Be careful, Bob. Give him something to hold on to.

Bob (*sarcastically*) Like what? Reins and harness?
Laura Turn your tie round and let him hold it.

Bob stops and does as instructed. Calvin, all pleased, shows the audience exactly what he has in mind for Bob. With menace, he recommences jumping up and down while kicking his heels into Bob's side. Suddenly, and with the utmost delight, he deliberately begins pulling harder and harder on the tie, causing it to become tighter and tighter around Bob's neck. Throughout the ride, Laura chips in with the odd word of encouragement and warning for the baby, failing to notice Bob's ordeal as he clutches at the tie in a desperate attempt for relief

He's really loving it, Bob. You must have a way with kids.
Bob (*hoarsely*) Get ... get ... get him off me.

Eventually, exhausted and almost choking to death, Bob collapses in a heap, gasping for breath, throwing Calvin to the ground. Calvin climbs back on and again pulls harder at the tie and spurs into his side in a vain bid to induce him

Laura (*moving down*) That's enough Calvin, Uncle Bobby's tired now.

She helps Calvin off and starts to lead him back to the sofa, but he breaks away and gets on to Bob's back

Bob Laura!
Laura (*to Calvin*) Does Calvy want his bot-bots?
Bob Laura!

Helping Calvin off again, she guides him to the sofa and picks up the baby's bottle as Calvin struggles on to the sofa all contented

Laura (*handing him the bottle*) There's a clever Calvy.

Meanwhile, Bob slowly scrambles to his feet with his tie still hanging down his back, where it remains for the duration of the play, and staggers over to the sofa

(*To Bob*) Look at him drink, Bob. All that playing's made him thirsty.

Bob looks first at her and then towards the audience, with complete stupefaction across his face. Holding the small of his back, he leans down, extracts a can of lager from the plastic bag and flops down on the sofa

Bob Never again. Never ever again. (*He gestures to the can*) I deserve this.

The phone rings. Laura takes the can away and hands Bob the bottle, absentmindedly giving the can to Calvin

Laura You carry on feeding him while I get the phone.

She rises, crosses to the phone and lifts the receiver as Bob slides effortlessly into her seat, takes the can away from Calvin, placing it between them, and unceremoniously pushes the bottle into Calvin's mouth

Hallo, double five-two-seven-eight-six. Sorry? I can't hear you. ... You'll have to speak up—Who? ... Oh Katie. How's it going? (*She raises her voice*) I said how's it going? ... He's fine, Bob's been playing with him. ... I know, I didn't either.
Bob (*mumbling to himself*) I don't.
Laura Calvin's really taken to him. It's as though he's always known him.

Calvin almost chokes on his bottle

No, don't worry. As soon as he's finished his bottle we'll put him down for the night.

Calvin stops drinking and turns to Bob with the bottle still in his mouth. Bob, in return, stares back with a broad triumphant smile and with a single finger tilts the bottle higher

Bob Drink it all up.

Laura Well, don't keep thinking of him. ... Of course you're not wrong for leaving him. ... Don't be silly, relax and enjoy yourself. Have you met any hunky men there? ... Really, you'll have to tell me all about it when you get home, if you're still sober that is. ... Yes, baby's being good, he's a little angel. Bob's giving him his bottle. ... I know.

Bob suddenly screams out loud as Calvin spits a mouthful of milk down his expensive shirt. Laura reels around at the commotion as Bob leaps to his feet

Bob Arrrgh!!

Laura What was what? (*She plays for time*) Sorry, you'll have to speak up, it's all the noise in the background. ... Oh, that was just Bob and Calvin playing. (*She covers the phone with her hand*) Be quiet, she can hear you. (*To Katie*) They're enjoying themselves enormously.

Bob Tell her what this little git's just done.

During the following, Calvin, unnoticed, picks up the can of lager and begins shaking it vigorously

Laura That was Bob. He said to tell you that it was just a bit of fun. Better go now, see you later. ... Bye. (*She replaces the receiver. Curtly*) Have you gone mad! She's worried enough as it is, without you shouting out stupid comments. Do you want her to think we can't cope—we're incompetent?

Bob Look what he's done to my shirt. Have you any idea how much it cost?

Laura It's your own fault, you played too rough with him. That's why he was sick.

Bob He wasn't sick, he did it on purpose. That little monster knew
   precisely what he was doing.
Laura (*incredulously*) You're pathetic! How can you say that?
Bob Because it's true.
Laura You're unbelievable. (*She holds out her hand*) Give me the
   shirt, I'll pop it in the washing machine.

*Bob removes the shirt, leaving his tie still around his neck, and
hands it to her*

Laura half snatches it and exits DR

*Calvin, who has been shaking the can of lager continuously, quickly
sets the can down, just as Bob turns round and picks it up again*

Bob (*to himself, opening the can*) It's not how I'd envisaged she'd
   get my shirt off tonight. (*He pulls back the can tab and his face
   and hair are instantly sprayed with the exploding lager*)

*Calvin laughs and bounces with joy on the sofa. With controlled
patience, Bob places the can beside the sofa and stands leering
down at Calvin, waiting for his laughter to subside, which gradually
it does as he realizes Bob's thunderous mood*

Pause

Right, you little shit. Now you just listen to me. You've had your
fun, and it's over. When she comes back I want you to drink that
bottle, get into your cot, and if I hear so much as a mouse's fart
creaking from your bedroom, I'm going to come in there and stick
your dummy where the light don't shine. Do I make myself clear?
(*He extracts the packet of contraceptives from behind the cushion
and waves them about*) Six years! Six years I've waited for a
chance like this, and no pint-sized spoilt brat of an infant is going
to mess it up. Do you hear me?

Laura enters from DR

Bob quickly hides the packet behind his back, backing up in front of the sofa

Laura Your shirt's in the wash, I put it in with two tea towels I found that were dirty. What've you got behind your back?
Bob Behind my back?
Laura Yes, I saw you put something behind your back as I came in.
Bob Oh, behind my back you mean. Just one of Alvin's toys.
Laura Calvin. His name's *Calvin*.

Calvin positions himself behind Bob and bites his finger, forcing him to drop the packet

Bob (*wildly*) Ouch! The little bastard bit me!
Laura (*offended*) Don't swear at him.
Bob Oh, I'll thank him, shall I? For severing my finger at the knuckle.

Quickly picking up the packet, Calvin puts it between his lips and lowers himself down on to the floor

Laura Now he's got something in his mouth.
Bob Probably my fingers.
Laura It looks like a packet of something.

She starts towards Calvin but Bob is first to react

Bob (*quickly*) I'll get it. (*He reaches down*)

Calvin's too fast and moves away. Bob tries desperately to retrieve the packet, but Calvin continually evades him and the chase extends all around the room until Calvin accidentally crashes against Laura's legs. Tugging frantically at her dress, he makes her take the packet from his mouth. Parking himself in front of the sofa between the two, he sits back with a smile of self-righteous satisfaction to follow the subsequent dialogue intensely, moving his head from one to the other and reacting accordingly

Laura (*reading the packet*) What's this?

Bob (*innocently*) Don't know.

Laura They're contraceptives!

Bob (*with mock surprise*) Are they? Must be Katie's.

Laura (*amazed*) Katie's!

Bob Why not? Single woman, own flat, already got a child. Makes sense to take precautions. Silly place to leave them though.

Laura (*suspiciously*) Where?

Bob Under the cushion. (*He realizes his mistake*) That's where they were ... under the cushion.

Laura Then why were you trying to hide them? If they were Katie's?

Bob Er ... blushes... To save Katie's ... no, *your* blushes... Well, both your blushes actually.

Laura You're waffling.

Bob No, I'm not.

Laura What do you take me for? These aren't Katie's, they're yours.

Bob (*with a smile of piousness*) Mine? Now I ask you, what would I be doing with those?

Laura Don't you mean "what would I be doing with those *tonight*"?

Bob (*dismissively*) Same thing.

Laura No, it's not, Bob. Besides, Katie's stayed in every night since the baby's been born. She hasn't had a boyfriend. So that makes these rather superfluous, doesn't it?

Bob Maybe she felt lucky tonight.

Laura You bought them purposely, didn't you?

Bob I told you. They're not mine.

Laura (*reading the packet*) OK. So, tell me Mister I've-Got-All-The-Answers. What would Katie be doing with ones that glow in the dark?

Bob Maybe she thought there'd be a power cut, I don't know.

Laura I know they're yours. Don't compound it by lying. What do you take me for? No, don't answer that, I already know. (*She holds up the packet*) An easy target. Another notch on your headboard, a scalp for your trophy room.

Bob (*conceding defeat*) All right, they're mine! But it's only a packet of contraceptives. It shows consideration.

Laura It shows intent.

Bob Yes, I intended to be considerate.

Laura (*sarcastically*) You were thinking of me. Aren't I silly, I should've known you wouldn't be thinking of yourself.

Bob I don't see why you're getting so uptight. It's what babysitting is all about. Surely you knew that?

Laura No, Bob, I didn't. I foolishly believed it was about looking after babies.

Bob Well, it is at first, until they go to bed. (*To Calvin*) With normal babies, that is.

Laura And then we leap on the sofa, is that it?

Bob I thought that's why you invited me along.

Laura I invited you along for moral support. Nothing else.

Bob Well, you didn't display many morals earlier, before the baby woke up.

Laura Bob, I was fighting you off, not egging you on.

Bob You didn't seem to be fighting very hard to me. (*He points at Calvin*) In fact, if it wasn't for that little trouble maker...

Laura And that's another thing ... your jealousy.

Bob (*astonished*) Jealous! Of *him* ... *Malvin*! You're joking.

Laura You can't even get his name right. It's Calvin with a C.

Bob Whatever.

Laura I've seen and heard how you've been with him.

The front door slams shut off stage and Katie enters UL

Bob Do you wonder why, what he's put me through. And what do I get out of it ... nothing.

Katie Hi, I had to come home, I couldn't enjoy myself for worrying. Donna's still there.

Bob Good. I think I'll join her.

Katie (*sensing the atmosphere*) What's going on?

Bob We're having a disagreement about your sweet little baby.

Katie Why? What's he done?

Laura Nothing.

Bob Oh really, let's recap, shall we? He's smeared food all over me, sprayed beer in my face, ruined my suit, spewed down my shirt, pulled clumps out of my hair, bruised my ribs and nearly broken my back. Not to mention severing my fingers with his teeth and almost choking me to death.

Katie looks bemused at Laura

Laura (*shrugging her shoulders*) He was only playing.
Bob Well, I don't want to play any more. (*He mimicks a child*) "I'm taking my ball back". Could you kindly get my shirt and jacket, I'm leaving.
Laura (*venomously*) Fine.

Laura storms off DR

Katie stares at him rather peculiarly

Katie If he was that bad, why didn't you just give him some gripe water? That's what I do when he plays up. It always works. He can't stand it. I did tell Laura.
Bob (*mumbling to himself*) Oh, did you? Right, that does it.

Katie exits DR

Bob crosses to the play-pen, leans over and picks up Calvin's teddy

(*To Calvin*) I'll wipe that smug smile off your face. (*He pulls the head off the teddy, holds it up in a taunting fashion and then tosses both parts back into the play-pen. He sneers*) No favourite toy any more ... all gone. *And* you'll get the blame. (*He looks skyward*) Revenge is mine.
Calvin (*to the audience*) Didn't like the toy anyway. It was Mum's favourite, not mine. She always put it beside me. Wait till she sees what he's done. He never wins—always loses. I'm glad. He shouldn't fight against me because we babies are never wrong. We don't know what we're doing, do we?

As Bob moves above the sofa, he accidentally kicks the bottle of gripe water which is lying on the floor

Bob What's this? (*He picks up the bottle and a table spoon lying close by*) Gripe water. (*He moves in front of the sofa towards Calvin*)

Seeing the bottle, Calvin starts to back up slowly

Oh, no, you don't, my friend. (*Kneeling down, he prevents Calvin from crawling away*) It's almost as if you knew what you've been doing tonight. (*Looking hard into his face*) You did know, didn't you?

Laura enters DR, *carrying his dripping wet shirt in one hand and his jacket in the other*

Laura (*crossing*) Here's your shirt, still wet, I'm afraid. (*She throws the shirt on to his bare torso*)

Bob stiffens with the sudden coldness

And your jacket. (*She throws it down hard on top of the shirt*) Your package is inside. I've no doubt Donna will appreciate it. (*She moves* DL, *crossing her arms and waiting for Bob to leave*)

Bob regains his composure after the sudden shock, slowly unscrews the bottle top and carefully pours a spoonful of gripe water

Katie enters DR

Katie What are you doing?
Bob (*looking up at her*) Just giving Calvin some of his *own* medicine. (*With a swift movement, he pours the gripe water into Calvin's mouth*)

With terror and disgust Calvin shouts for his mother

Calvin (*screaming*) Mummmmy!!

They all freeze at this unexpected utterance of his first word. Calvin, realizing what he has done, covers his mouth with his hand and stares towards the audience in horror and disbelief as——

                              —the CURTAIN *falls*

FURNITURE AND PROPERTY LIST

Further dressing may be added at the director's discretion

SCENE 1

On stage: Large play-pen. *In it:* nursery book, baby's rattle, small
         teddy bear, various coloured plastic bricks (2 red and
         2 yellow)
         Sofa with matching cushions
         Replica antique table. *On it:* telephone, address book
         Coat stand
         Large cardboard box containing toys
         Standard lamp
         Rocking chair
         Inexpensive bookcase
         Baby toys, baby clothes, and strewn newspaper on floor

Off stage: Hair brush (**Katie**)
         Carrier bag. *In it:* 4 cans of lager and a bottle of wine (**Bob**)
         Shoes (**Katie**)

Personal: **Katie:** large bath towel
         Calvin: dummy on ribbon
         Bob: comb, small portable cassette player, small roll-on
         deodorant, bottle of aftershave, breath freshener spray,
         packet of contraceptives, handkerchief

SCENE 2

Set: Wine glass
     Empty wine bottle

Rattle behind cushions on sofa
Two empty lager cans
Toys on floor
2 coloured plastic toy bricks in front of sofa

Off stage: Large baby doll wrapped in blanket (**Laura**)
Basket of nappy change items including hidden bottle of
  gripe water and spoon (**Bob**)
Plastic dish of baby food, spoon (**Bob**)
Baby's bottle (**Laura**)

LIGHTING PLOT

Property fittings required: nil
Interior. The same throughout

SCENE 1. Early evening

To open: Overall general lighting

Cue 1   **Bob** sings "Tell Laura I love her"   (Page 17)
                Black-out

SCENE 2. Evening

To open: Overall general lighting

Cue 2   **Bob** dims lights   (Page 18)
                Fade lights down

Cue 3   **Laura** switches lights to full   (Page 22)
                Bring up lights to full

Cue 4   **Calvin** stares at the audience   (Page 40)
                Black-out

EFFECTS PLOT

Cue 11   **Bob**: "I deserve this."   (Page 32)
             Phone rings

Cue 12   **Laura**: "…how you've been with him."   (Page 37)
             Sound of front door slamming shut

Lightning Source UK Ltd.
Milton Keynes UK
UKOW06f2043110216

268196UK00001B/6/P